D1155209

D.I.Y. MAKE IT HAPPEN

FANTASY FOOTBALL LEAGUE

VIRGINIA LOH-HAGAN

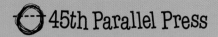
45th Parallel Press

Published in the United States of America by Cherry Lake Publishing
Ann Arbor, Michigan
www.cherrylakepublishing.com

Content Adviser: Michael Rockett, Fantasy Football team owner, Ypsilanti, Michigan
Reading Adviser: Marla Conn, ReadAbility, Inc.
Book Designer: Felicia Macheske

Photo Credits: © Pete Saloutos/Shutterstock.com, cover, 1; © Africa Studio/Shutterstock.com, 3, 31; © Richard Paul Kane/Shutterstock.com, 5; © Wayne0216/Shutterstock.com, 7; © Steve Debenport/iStock, 9; © Dmitry Kalinovsky/Shutterstock.com, 10; © Pamela Moore/iStock, 12, 18; © Samuel Borges Photography/Shutterstock.com, 19; © wavebreakmedia/Shutterstock.com, 15, 27, 31, back cover; © Monkey Business Images/Shutterstock.com, 16; © Beto Chagas/Shutterstock.com, 17, 30; © ostill/Shutterstock.com, 20; © Felix Mizioznikov/Shutterstock.com, 23; © blueflames/iStock, 25; © nullplus/iStock, 28; © Dora Zett/Shutterstock.com, back cover

Graphic Elements: pashabo/Shutterstock.com, 6, back cover; axako/Shutterstock.com, 7; © dapoomll/Shutterstock.com, 7; IreneArt/Shutterstock.com, 4, 8; bokasin/Shutterstock.com, 11, 19; © Iriskana/Shutterstock.com, 11, 19; Belausava Volha/Shutterstock.com, 12, 20; Nik Merkulov/Shutterstock.com, 13; Ya Tshey/Shutterstock.com, 14, 27; kubais/Shutterstock.com, 15; Sasha Nazim/Shutterstock.coms, 17, 24; Ursa Major/Shutterstock.com, 23, 28; Infomages/Shutterstock.com, 26; © topform/Shutterstock, back cover; © Art'nLera/Shutterstock, back cover

45th Parallel Press is an imprint of Cherry Lake Publishing.

Library of Congress Cataloging-in-Publication Data

Loh-Hagan, Virginia.
  Fantasy football league / by Virginia Loh-Hagan.
     pages cm. — (D.I.Y. make it happen)
  Includes bibliographical references and index.
  ISBN 978-1-63470-499-1 (hardcover) — ISBN 978-1-63470-559-2 (pdf) — ISBN 978-1-63470-619-3 (paperback) — ISBN 978-1-63470-679-7 (ebook)
  1. Rotisserie League Football (Game)—Juvenile literature. I. Title.
  GV1202.F34L64 2016
  794.8'63326406—dc23
                              2015026846

Cherry Lake Publishing would like to acknowledge the work of The Partnership for 21st Century Skills.
Please visit *www.p21.org* for more information.

Printed in the United States of America
Corporate Graphics Inc.

ABOUT THE AUTHOR

Dr. Virginia Loh-Hagan is an author, university professor, former classroom teacher, and curriculum designer. She's not a football fan. But she loves football party food. She lives in San Diego with her very tall husband and very naughty dogs. To learn more about her, visit www.virginialoh.com.

TABLE OF CONTENTS

CHAPTER ONE

WHAT DOES IT MEAN TO START A FANTASY FOOTBALL LEAGUE?

Do you love football? Do you love playing games? Do you love planning? Then starting a fantasy football league is the right project for you!

Football is a sport. There are two teams. There are 11 players on each team. They play on a field. There are end zones at each end. Players get the ball into the end zone. They score points. The team with the most points wins.

Fantasy football is a contest. People create fake teams. They select players from the NFL (National Football League). They score points based on how players do in real games. A fantasy football **league** is a group of people. They play fantasy football.

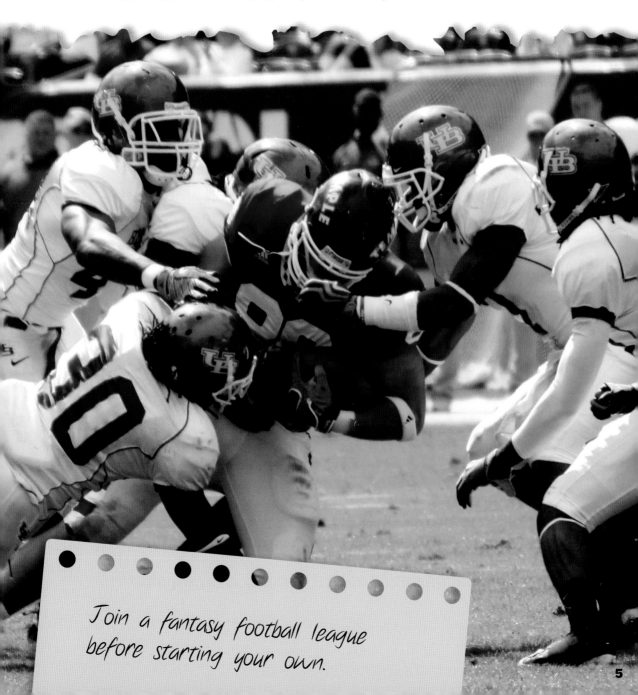

Join a fantasy football league before starting your own.

KNOW THE LINGO

Breakout: when a player goes from okay to great

Bust: a player who performs well below expectations

Collusion: two owners working together to win a league

Damaged goods: when a player involved in a trade gets hurt

Drop: cutting a player from your roster

Elite: the highest-ranked players at their positions

Fire sale: when owners trade their players after losing a season to help another team win the championship

Fleecing: taking advantage of an owner in a trade

Handcuffing: drafting a backup and starter from the same NFL team

IR (injured reserve): a player who is currently injured and takes up a spot on the roster

Private league: a league that can only be joined by invitation

Public league: a league that anyone can join

Sleeper: a player who exceeds expectations; an underdog

Stud: a top-rated starter

Trade bait: good players that owners can offer to other owners

Fantasy football is popular in the fall. That's football season.

People start fantasy football leagues for several reasons. They like competing. They like pretending to be team **owners**. Owners are people who manage a team. They learn more about the sport and players. They like math. It makes watching football more exciting.

People also make money. Most leagues charge a **fee**. A fee is the cost. Part of the fee goes toward prizes. People can win the money.

Starting a fantasy football league is a good idea. You can hang out with friends. You can make new friends. You can watch a lot of football.

Practice math, especially statistics.

CHAPTER TWO

WHAT DO YOU NEED TO START A FANTASY FOOTBALL LEAGUE?

A fantasy football league needs members.

➡ Get people. Ask friends. Ask classmates. Ask neighbors. Each person owns a team. League members are called owners.

➡ Create 8 to 12 teams. Twelve teams is ideal. Get an even number of teams. Odd numbers are hard to schedule.

Appoint a **commissioner**. This person is the leader. This person does many things.

➡ **Takes care of arguments.**

➡ **Takes care of money.**

➡ **Keeps track of rosters. Rosters are lists of players.**

➡ **Keeps track of trades. Trades are when owners switch players.**

➡ **Keeps track of team standings. This is a list of teams' wins and losses.**

The commissioner makes the final decision when there are arguments.

9

Come up with names.

➡ **Name the league.**

➡ **Have owners name their teams.**

Decide how you want to deal with money. Some leagues play just for fun, not money.

➡ **Decide an entry fee. This is the cost of joining.**

➡ **Decide how much money goes into the pot. The pot is the prize money. It's for the winners. Decide how to divide the prize money.**

➡ **Use the money to pay for snacks and supplies for your league.**

Think of creative team names.

Set up the schedule.

➡ **Plan for 15-17 weeks. The NFL** season is 17 weeks long. Each **NFL** team has one week off. It's called a **bye week**.

➡ **Decide match-ups.** A match-up is a pair of fantasy teams in your league. They will compete. Do this for each week.

➡ **Prepare for playoffs.** This is when the top fantasy teams play. They play for the championship. This is at the end of the season.

Learn about football. Learn about players. Learn game rules. Keep up with what's happening.

➡ **Watch football games.**

➡ **Read football articles.**

➡ **Talk to other football fans.**

➡ **Listen to sports talk shows.**

Get supplies for the **draft**. The draft is when owners choose players.

➡ **Consider getting a Web site. There are online tools. They help manage your league.**

➡ **Get food and snacks.**

➡ **Get poster board. Make a 6-inch column for each team. Write each team name at the top.**

➡ **Get pens and pencils.**

➡ **Get cards. Put the names of football players on them. Color-code them by position. Have owners select players.**

Get tips from other fantasy football leagues.

TRY THIS!

People get really excited about starting things. Weeks go by. They lose interest. They stop participating. The same thing can happen in a fantasy football league. Keep people interested. Offer prizes each week for different things. People like the chance of winning.

You'll need: prizes

Steps

1 Include costs of prizes in the fees. Or ask for donations. Donations are gifts of money.

2 Get prizes. Examples are snacks, school supplies, or movie tickets.

3 Think of different contests for each week. For example, in week one, award the owner with the best team name. In week two, award the owner who has the best sportsmanship. In week three, award the owner with the highest-scoring quarterback. In week four, award the owner with the lowest points.

4 At the beginning of the week, announce the contest.

5 At the end of the week, announce the winner. Give the prize.

CHAPTER THREE

HOW DO YOU SET UP A FANTASY FOOTBALL LEAGUE?

Create rules. Write them down.

➡ Decide how you want to score. Select points that owners get for each action. Actions include yards gained. They include touchdowns. Touchdowns are when a team gets to the end zone.

➡ Decide how teams get to the playoffs. Decide how many teams make the playoffs. Decide when those match-ups will be played.

➡ Decide rules for the waiver wire. This is how owners pick up free agents. Free agents are players who aren't on rosters. Decide rules for picking up players. Decide how many free agents a team can add. Decide the selection order.

➡ Decide the process for trades. Some leagues are allowed to veto a trade. Veto means deny.

MATTHEW BERRY

Matthew Berry is a senior fantasy sports analyst. He works for ESPN. He speaks on television. He speaks on the radio. He wrote a book about fantasy sports. It's called *Fantasy Life*. He advises practicing etiquette. Etiquette is proper behavior. It's rules for how people act and behave in a fantasy league. He has rules for talking with other owners. Here are some of his rules:

- Be clear. Be crystal clear.
- A negotiation should be between two teams and only two teams.
- Your word should mean something.
- Take no for an answer.
- Respond—even if it's with a simple yes or no.
- Everyone should be allowed to manage their own team their own way. Even if you don't agree with it. Even if it's done badly.
- Be human. This game should be fun.

Berry said, "It really comes back to the Golden Rule. ... Do unto others as you would have them do to you."

Remember that every league is different.

Decide how you want to fill team rosters.

➡ **Decide how many players.**

➡ **Decide which positions you want.**

➡ **Decide how many players per position.**

➡ **Decide if you want team defense or individual player defense. Team defenses score as 1 player.**

Learn about each player before making lineup decisions.

Study the players. Find out about players.

➡ **Watch pre-season football games.**

➡ **Read fantasy football Web sites.**

Bring cheat sheets. Cheat sheets are prepared lists of players. Players are ranked. They're in order of value.

Pick players you think will score points for you.

Prepare for the draft. This is a big event in fantasy football. Owners create their rosters. They take turns choosing players.

➡ **Choose a date. Do** it close to the start of football season.

➡ **Do a live event. Or** do an online event.

➡ **For live events, choose a place. Choose** a place available to you. **Examples** are homes or classrooms. **Most** league members want access to the Internet.

Owners select a player in each **round**.
A round is a turn.

➡ **Have owners pick numbers out of a hat. This decides the order owners will select.**

➡ **Set a time limit.**

➡ **Record picks on the poster board. Put the player's card under the team name.**

Tick
Tick
Tick

Bring a timer. People who take too long to pick players lose their turn.

Keep track of who's been picked and who hasn't.

Decide how you want to do your draft. There are different ways to do it.

➡ **There's a snake draft. In round one, teams 1 through 12 pick. They go in that order. In round two, team 12 picks first. Then, teams 11 through 1 pick. In round three, team 1 picks first again. Repeat the pattern.**

➡ **There's an auction draft. Owners bid for players. Each owner has a fake amount of money. Owners take turns. They choose players. They bid for them. High bids get the player. They bid until they run out of money.**

➡ **Some leagues do both. They auction for part of their roster. They snake the rest.**

➡ **There's autopick draft. Players are assigned to owners.**

There are ways to change the roster after the draft.

➡ **Pick up free agents. Drop a player on your roster. That makes room for the free agent.**

➡ **Trade players. Submit trades to the commissioner.**

Decide your standings plan. Decide your scoring plan. There are different plans.

Scoring points

➡ **There's points-per-reception. Points are given for each reception. That's when players catch the ball.**

➡ **There's pure scoring. Points are given for touchdowns. They're given for touchdown passes. They're given for field goals.**

➡ **There's pure yardage. Yardage is distance in yards. Points are given for passing. They're given for rushing. They're given for receiving yards.**

Standings

➡ **There's head-to-head. The starters' points are added up. The winning team from each match-up wins. Teams with the most wins make the play-offs.**

➡ **There's total points. Teams get points on an ongoing basis. Total the starters' points from all weeks. The top teams compete in playoffs.**

Or create your own scoring plan. This is **custom**-scoring. Custom means you design your own. Here's a common example:

➡ **Touchdowns are 6 points.**

➡ **Sacks, safeties, and turnovers are 2 points.**

➡ **10 rushing or receiving yards are 1 point.**

➡ **40 passing yards are 1 point.**

➡ **Interception thrown or fumble lost are -2 points.**

Consider giving bonus points.

CHAPTER FOUR

HOW DO YOU RUN A FANTASY FOOTBALL LEAGUE?

You've got members. You've got teams. You're ready for fantasy football. The most important event is draft day. There are many things you have to do.

➡ **Get some football decorations. Get owners excited.**

➡ **Prepare to spend three hours drafting.**

➡ **Introduce everybody. Encourage bragging. Encourage joking. It's part of fantasy football.**

➡ **Plan breaks. Have people move around. Have people talk about strategies.**

- Have owners talk about each other's picks.
- Create a game schedule.

QUICK TIPS

- People may cheat. Pay attention to all the teams. Watch trades.

- Recruit someone who's not in the league to help you. You may need a "neutral" perspective. This is someone who doesn't care whose team wins.

- Starting a league is a lot of work. Don't let your duties affect your own draft. Focus on building a strong team.

- During the draft, stay focused. Things happen quickly. Change your picks as needed.

- Focus on running backs. They're key point scorers.

- Do a mock draft. Mock means fake. This is for practice. Figure out a strategy.

- Don't drop rookies. Rookies are new players. It takes awhile for them to get good.

- Create a tradition. This builds community. An example is wearing matching hats on game days.

- Charge fines. Fines are charged for not doing something. An example is fining members for not setting their rosters. This may encourage people to participate in league activities.

To play, create a **lineup**. This is your play list. Do this before the match-up each week. It can change each week. But it's locked until the week's games are done.

➡ **Decide your starters. These players score fantasy points.**

➡ **Decide your bench players. These players aren't playing. But they're on your roster. They play if a starter is injured. They play if a starter has a bye week.**

Keep track of points. Do this at the end of the week's games. Change your team standings.

You will need to pay attention to NFL games every week.

There are many things to do during fantasy football season.

⇒ **Watch football games. Host game parties. Talk about the games.**

⇒ **Keep track of player injuries. Hurt players affect your roster. They affect your points.**

⇒ **Study players and teams. Keep track of their points. Use a free fantasy football Web site.**

Keep everyone happy. It's fun to play with the same people every year.

→ Send reports to owners. **Note team standings. Note who's in first place. Note who's in last place.**

→ **Keep track of trades. Make waiver wire lists.**

→ **Make sure owners follow rules.**

There are things to do after fantasy football season.

→ **Figure out everyone's points. Have someone double-check your math.**

→ **Announce winners. Give out prizes. Some leagues focus more on losers than winners. Losers have to do silly things.**

→ **Thank everyone for participating.**

→ **Tell owners to participate again next year.**

Starting a fantasy football league is a lot of work. But it's also a lot of fun!

D.I.Y. EXAMPLE!

STEPS	EXAMPLES
League name	Pigskin Justice League
Team name	Sandy Seahawks
Number of teams	12
Fee	$25 per team (Total: $300)
Expenses	$50 for supplies (draft board, snacks, drinks)
Prizes	Winner: $125; 2nd place: $75; 3rd place: $50
Team roster	<ul><li>1 quarterback</li><li>2 running backs</li><li>2 wide receivers</li><li>1 tight end</li><li>1 kicker</li><li>1 defense</li><li>6 bench players</li></ul>

STEPS	EXAMPLES
Scoring system	◆ 1 point for 25 passing yards
	◆ 1 point for 10 rushing yards
	◆ 1 point for 10 receiving yards
	◆ 6 points for a touchdown
	◆ 4 points for a passing touchdown
	◆ -2 points for every interception thrown or fumble lost
	◆ 1 point for each extra point made
	◆ 3 points for each 0- to 39-yard field goal, 4 points for each 40- to 49-yard field goal, and 5 points for each 50-plus-yard field goal
	◆ 2 points per turnover gained by defense
	◆ 1 point per sack by the defense
	◆ 2 points for a safety by defense
	◆ 6 points for each touchdown scored by defense
	◆ 2 points for each blocked kick

GLOSSARY

auction (AWK-shuhn) bidding

autopick (AW-toh-pik) when players are assigned to owners

bench players (BENCH PLAY-urz) players that aren't starting or playing

bye week (BYE WEEK) the week when the NFL team doesn't play

cheat sheets (CHEET SHEETS) prepared lists of players that are ranked by fantasy value

commissioner (kuh-MISH-uh-nur) leader

custom (KUHS-tuhm) designing your own thing

draft (DRAFT) event when owners choose players

fee (FEE) cost of joining

free agents (FREE AY-juhnts) players who aren't on rosters but are available to be picked up

league (LEEG) group of people with common interests

lineup (LINE-up) a list of players who are playing

match-up (MACH uhp) a pair of fantasy teams that compete

owners (OHN-urz) members of a fantasy football league who manage teams

playoffs (PLAY-awfs) the top teams competing for the championship

pot (PAHT) money from owners put into a collection for prizes

reception (ri-SEP-shuhn) catching a ball

rosters (RAH-sturz) lists of players on a team

round (ROUND) a turn for each owner

standings (STAN-dingz) list of each teams' wins and losses

starters (STAHRT-urz) players who are playing

touchdowns (TUHCH-dounz) goals in football

trades (TRAYDZ) switching players

veto (VEE-toh) to deny, to not allow

waiver wire (WAY-vur WIRE) group of free agents waiting to be picked up by team owners

yardage (YAHRD-idj) distance in yards

INDEX

LEARN MORE

BOOKS

Jacobs, Greg. *The Everything Kids' Football Book*. Avon, MA: Adams Media, 2014.

Signore, Martin. *Fantasy Football for Dummies*. Indianapolis, IN: Wiley Pub., Inc. 2007.

WEB SITES

Fantasy Sports Trade Association: www.fsta.org

Fleaflicker—Free and Easy Fantasy Football: www.fleaflicker.com

Sports Illustrated Kids—Blogs: Fantasy Fix: www.sikids.com/blogs/fantasy%20fix